Thirty Days to a Thankful Body

(A Body Full of Thanks)

Nagueyalti Warren, PhD

The inspiration for this book came to me while I was deep in Spirit—inspired, that is, but not in meditation; rather, I was immersed in a bathtub of brilliant bubbles soaking and relaxing in perfectly warmed water. I had just hung up from a telephone conversation with a good friend who was nervously awaiting the results of some test to see if she had cancer.

As I scrubbed my feet, I felt an overwhelming sense of gratitude for what feet actually do day after day. Then a light went on. I realized that each part of the body performs it function repeatedly and usually without thanks. I wondered what a well-thanked body would feel like. So everyday for thirty days, I made a concerted effort to say thanks and to send love to each part of my body. The results? I felt great. I felt loved and loving.

I hope that you have selected this book because you want to feel better in your body than you do currently. While I cannot offer a guarantee, I do believe and feel certain that if you follow the daily rituals, saying thank you to all of your body parts, you will produce a wonderful peaceful feeling that is so satisfying. In addition, this is a great way to get in touch with your body. Take one body part each day. Say the blessings aloud. Either say or write the affirmations. As you believe in your heart, so it is.

This book is not intended to diagnose or treat any illness. If you discover anything unusual as you pay attention to your body, please see a licensed physician or other health care provider.

Day One

Bless my feet! Today I give thanks for my feet. They have walked with me all the days of my life. They have carried me from childhood, supported all my weight, even my overweight. Thank you feet for loving me. I bless you for a job well done. I bless every corn. Each corn is an expression of your love for me, an effort to protect me. I bless each toe. Each toe helps me to stand, balance and walk. Thank you feet for dancing. Thank you toenails for protecting my toes.

Forgive me if I have made you wear shoes too small, too tight or heels too high.

Thank you feet; you are so sweet. You hold my sole, and keep me in touch with mother earth.

If you have no feet, thank the idea of feet and the wonderful inventors who have searched for suitable substitute feet—creating crutches, artificial feet, and wheelchairs. Thank those substitutes that carry you around for these **have a new kind of soul.**

Love Recipe for your soles

1 cup of raw honey
2 tablespoons of apple cider vinegar
2 tablespoons of olive oil
Heat until the ingredients are blended. Then set aside to cool.
Soak feet in warm water mixed with 2 cups whole milk and 2 cups

Epson Salt
Soak feet for at least 20 minutes; use a loofah to remove dead skin.
Pat dry, then apply the honey mixture.
Massage it into feet and relax while it works.
Rinse feet in milk water. Pat dry. Apply your favorite lotion.

Footnote:
Paint each toenail a different color, men too. Don't let women have all the fun!

Affirmation: My feet are now perfect, whole, and complete.

Day Two

Bless my ankles! My ankles are the joints! I bless the connection from my feet to my legs. My ankles are hinges that work perfectly. Thank you ankle; may you be ever strong and stand by me. I love you and I appreciate you.

If you have a broken ankle or a sprained ankle, tell it to heal. It can and will. If you have an artificial ankle, praise it and its inventor for filling in for the real one.

Are your ankles rusty? You know, ashy and uncared for. Today is be kind to your ankles day. Rub them with some baby oil or olive oil and watch them bless you.

Affirmation: My ankles are right now strong and healthy, sleek and beautiful.

Day Three

I bless you lower legs. My legs are lovely. They hold me up. I thank you two bones: the fibula and tibia. All praise to the fibula and the tibia. Thank you for your strength and your faithfulness. I thank you muscles that cover these bones and I thank and love you skin and shin.

If these bones are not healthy, thank them anyway and ask them to get better. Tell the bones that you know their pain and that you love them anyway and want what is best for them. Thank them sincerely.

Massage your legs with a mixture of warm olive oil and several drops of Geranium tincture. As you massage speak kindly and lovingly to your lower legs.

Affirmation: My lower legs are right here and right now in perfect health, and are long, lean and lovely or thick, strong, and husky or smooth or hairy. It does not matter. They are alive and well.

Day Four

Thank you knees. Bless you for supporting almost all of my body weight. Forgive me for excess weight. I am truly sorry if I have overburdened you. I love you and promise to take off the weight. You have been a true friend holding me up in spite of my excess, and I have not taken the time to say thank you. Thank you. You are an amazing joint.

If your knees hurt, give them a break; take off the weight. If you have an artificial knee, praise science and your surgeon.

Rub your knees with warm castor oil and kiss them goodnight. In the morning they will thank you and your skin will feel soft and smooth.

Affirmation: My knees know how to bend and stretch and are strong and healthy. My knees know and it is so; I kneel on my knees and bless each cell, fiber, and nerve.

Day Five

I thank you thighs. You hold the longest and strongest bones in my body. The femur connects my lower body to my upper body, and you join me at my hips; a ball and socket deal. I appreciate all that you do for me. Forgive me if I have neglected you. My muscles may be slack and my thigh skin flabby or perhaps I have covered you in cellulite. Forgive me. I do love you and I promise to exercise and tighten you up. You are so helpful to me. Thanks!

A Mixture for Loving and Thanking Thighs

1 cup of witch hazel
1 cup of wintergreen alcohol
1 cup Epson Salts
¾ cup of olive oil
Mix together and rub into thighs, especially around cellulite and fat pockets. As you rub, tell your thighs how lovely they are and focus on how grateful you are to have them. Rinse off in warm bath or shower. Pat dry and follow with your favorite lotion.

Affirmation: My thighs are perfect, whole and complete. I claim perfect health for my thighs. My thighs are the perfect size. (If you think they are too fat or too skinny, look past the appearance and claim for yourself the perfect thigh).

Day Six

Thank goodness for the hippest hips in the world. I love you hips. Hip, hip hooray! Thank you for all that you do for me. You are my multi-axial joint, a ball and socket that lets me turn, flex and extend myself. Bless you hips.

If you have a hip replacement, thank the invention and the inventor. If you have hip pain, see your physician and don't be afraid to say goodbye to your hurting hip and trade it in for a new one! Thank goodness for science, the science of health.

Affirmation: My hips are strong and healthy. I exercise my hips with yoga stretches, and my hips move with ease and grace.

Day Seven

I thank you pelvis. Thanks, for all that you hold together. Thank you for growing as I have grown. I love you, I appreciate you, and I am thankful for you. Bone of my bone, flesh of my flesh, thanks for being the best. I give praise to my pelvis!

Affirmation: My pelvis is precious, whole, holy and complete. I claim perfection right here and right now!

Day Eight

Thank you reproductive organs. Thank you for carrying my children or for carrying the potential for children. (And if these organs no longer work, thank them for the times when they did). I praise the idea of what you do. I love the space where you are or were. I am grateful that some reproductive organs held on to me and brought me forth at the right time. Bless you for the spirit of reproduction.

Affirmation: My reproductive organs are life affirming, sacrosanct and highly respected.

Day Nine

Thank you abdomen. Yes! And I bless you lower belly.

(If it's out of shape, do sit ups and crunches).

Thank you abdomen and the button that connected me to my mother and nourished me in the womb. I rid myself of belly fat. (Your abdomen will thank you for it).

Affirmation: My lower belly is firm and tight. My abdomen is flat and smooth.

Day Ten

Thank you navel. Umbilical cord, lifeline—my place of connection to my mother, thanks lifeline.

Regardless of our relationship now, be it good or bad, I am thankful for the connection to life that she and her body provided for me. Thanks mom for not cutting me loose until the right time. As I place my hand to my navel, I remember my connection to you.

I love you navel, my point of no return. I thank you for the nourishment that you provided for me when I could not provide it for myself.

Affirmation: Today I thank my navel, the place where I come together, the place where I disconnected, and the center of me. Today I meditate on my navel and find peace.

Day Ten

Thank you stomach. My bread basket. (Kiss it if you can). I love you and thank you for breaking down my food into nutrients that I can use.

The word stomach in French translates as *stoma* or mouth. It is the cavity where most food that you eat gets broken down by stomach acids. However, a more interesting definition is one in the *Webster Unabridged Dictionary*. Stomach as a verb is "To remember with anger; to take offence; enrage; irritate; to put up with or to bear without overt resentment. Your stomach is the mouth or the opening of your emotions. To get down in the mouth is actually to be down in your stomach! Thus, butterflies in the stomach are a clue to your emotional compass. When they flutter in your stomach listen and lighten up. Calm down. Take deep breaths. Smile. Tell your stomach that you love all that it does for you.

Exercise for the stomach: place your hand on your stomach and rub clockwise to the count of 50. Then reverse and rub counter clockwise for the count of 50. This is a Chinese exercise said to be healing. Your stomach will enjoy the loving touch, and while I make no medical claims for its effects, it certainly will not hurt you.

Affirmation: Today I send love and light to my stomach. I promise to put only the healthiest foods and water into my stomach today. I will not stuff my stomach today.

Day Eleven

Thank you pancreas. Thank you for balancing my glucose level. Thanks for all the enzymatic work that you do for me. I love you.

If you have diabetes, be thankful for insulin and other medicines available to help you. Take your medication, check your glucose level, exercise and eat the appropriate foods.

Affirmation: I love and care for my body. Today I eliminate refined sugar and white flour from my diet. I eat whole grains, fruits, vegetables and drink pure water.

Day Twelve

I thank you kidneys and bladder. Thanks for filtering the waste from my body and thanks bladder for holding it until I expel the waste. I love and bless you both today.

The kidneys are twin organs that cleanse the blood. If your kidneys need help, be thankful for dialysis and transplants. Once thought to be the center of conscience, the kidneys actually do act as gatekeeper for what is right and wrong for the body.

Affirmation: I love and protect my kidneys and bladder. Today I drink plenty of fresh water and flush my kidneys and bladder.

Day Thirteen

Thank you liver and gall bladder. Liver you work hard with my metabolism, synthesizing my blood protein, and helping to detoxify my body. You are amazing! You can make yourself out of yourself. Dear gall bladder thanks for dissolving cholesterol and fat.

The liver is the only internal organ that can regenerate itself to a large extent. Connotatively the liver is sometimes called the seat of anger. Massage your liver and gall bladder by placing your hands on your stomach, under your rib cage and rub counter clockwise for the count of fifty, then reverse the motion for another count of fifty telling these organs that you love and appreciate them.

Affirmation: My liver and gall bladder are in perfect health. I am grateful for the part they play in my body. I love my liver.

Day Fourteen

Thank you lungs for breathing. I breathe in the holy breath of Spirit that gives breath to all alike. From the first breath, to the last you are my steady twins working hard. Thanks lungs for all you do for me.

If you have abused your lungs, knowingly or unknowingly by smoking or by inhaling toxins, you must ask your lung's forgiveness. Tell your lungs that you love them and that you never meant to harm them.

Imagine your lungs pink and healthy. Surround them in a warm glowing golden light. Repeat three times: I love my lungs, I love my lungs, I love my lungs.

Give thanks for the inventors of the iron lung, the respirator, and the ventilator invented to help the lungs breathe and to support life. Also thank the yogi for discovering the Breath of Fire: short pumping breaths that can charge your energy flow.

Affirmation: Today I breathe out toxins and I breathe in pure air, joy and peace. What I appreciate appreciates. My lungs are strong and healthy.

Day Fifteen

Bless you ribcage. I bless the bones that protect my heart and lungs. The seven pairs of ribs connected to my sternum are true ribs. The other three are called false ribs. I love all of you ribs true and false.

Rib as verb can mean to make fun of, to joke or to banter. Laughter is a great way to thank your ribs for holding you together. Laugh out loud and long every day regardless of whether or not you see humor. Make believe.

Affirmation: Today I find something to laugh about, something to tickle my rib bones. My ribs are strong and healthy and I exercise (lift weights) in order to keep them that way. I feed my bones calcium rich food and send love to my rib cage.

Day Sixteen

Well bless my heart! Bless you heart. I love your red, red blood bumping through my veins to your own very natural rhythm. I love you heart of mine.

The heart is a pump that circulates your blood, your life force. The heart also connotes love, courage, enthusiasm, intense concern, and one's innermost or actual character. Love your heart and see it surrounded in a golden healing light.

If you have heart trouble, practice forgiveness of self and of others. Every day forgive the little things and the big things. Forgive yourself your imperfections and forgive others theirs. Do not let your heart be troubled. You can do this by not taking anything personally. If your heart is diseased, give thanks for the artificial heart and heart transplants, and pacemakers. Be thankful for all the efforts made to save hearts.

Affirmation: Today I forgive myself for all my mistakes, I forgive others for theirs, and I accept forgiveness. I know that the Great Spirit holds no malice toward me or anyone else. I am free and my heart is at peace.

.

Day Seventeen

Bless you breasts. Thank you for your awesome potential in providing nourishment to infants. Thank you for supporting new life.

The word breast also connotes information, as in to be kept abreast of something. Keep abreast of your own breasts. Examine them, love them, talk to them and tell them to be well.

Men bless your chest. Bless that part of you that may also have breasts that need to be checked.

Affirmation: Today I bathe my breasts in the golden light of love. I stay abreast of their condition through monthly self-exams and yearly mammograms if I am forty and older.

❧

Day Eighteen

I thank you and thump you thymus. Thank you thymus for protecting me from infections every day of my life. I love you. I adore you.

The thymus is located behind the breastbone. If you have or suffer from infections, thank your thymus for keeping you from succumbing. By thumping lightly with your middle finger, you tell the thymus hello, to wake up and be active. The word thymus from the Greek *thymos* means to go deeper. In Sanskrit *dhuma* is the term related to thymus. It means to rise into flames and thus claims a spiritual connotation. So let your spirit rise.

The thymus wasn't even discovered until 1961! Still it was there doing its work all the time whether we were aware of it or not. Now that you know it's there, show it some love.

Affirmation: I love and thump my thymus. I love and appreciate all that the thymus does; its healing flame warms and protects me.

Day Nineteen

Thank you pituitary and pineal glands. Thank you for enabling me to grow, pituitary gland, and for controlling my blood pressure. Thank you pineal gland for the melatonin that you provide.

Some people think that the pineal gland is the third eye that provides spiritual insight.

Affirmation: I give great thanks and joy for the perfect functioning of all my endocrine glands.

Day Twenty

Thank you larynx—my voice box and my windpipe. Thanks for making noise before I could talk. Thanks for giving me voice and song. I love you. I bless you.

If you have lost your voice, apologize for anything you have done knowing or unknowingly to hurt your larynx. Thank and send love to the inventor of the electro-larynx.

Affirmation: My larynx is healthy and strong. My voice that can sing and talk is powerful. I am grateful for the artificial larynx.

Day Twenty-One

Thank you thyroid gland. I love you. I bless you, and I appreciate you and all that you do.

Thyroid in Greek means shield. Your thyroid is a shield of protection and energy (metabolism).

Hold your neck and send love to this endocrine gland. If your gland needs help to work properly, show gratitude for thyroxin, medicine for the proper function of this gland.

Affirmation: My thyroid gland works perfectly. It is perfect, whole and complete.

Day Twenty-Two

Bless my hands and arms. Thanks hands that lend help to others and that shake other hands in friendship. Thanks arms that hug me and those I love. Thanks for helping me carry in the shopping bags and books. Thanks for helping me wave goodbye and hello. I adorn you with jewelry, rings, bracelets and watches. I am so grateful for these appendages.

If you have a missing limb, be thankful for prosthetics.

Affirmation: My hands and arms are loved and lovely. They are healthy and helpful.

❧

Day Twenty-Three

Thank you eyes. I see the beauty of the world. I see the beautiful spirit in each and every human being, plant, animal and every living creature. I thank you each eyeball and my eyelashes and eyebrows that protect them. I thank you eyes for the full color views of sunsets, moon risings, rainbows, roses and trees. I love you.

If you do not have 20/20 vision, be thankful for corrective lenses and eye surgery. Give your eyes a break. For a soothing treatment and to say thanks for eyes, slice a chilled cucumber and place a slice on each closed eyelid as you recline in a relaxing position. Spend thirty minutes in this position, all the while telling your eyes thanks.

Affirmation: My eyes are my windows on a beautiful world. I am thankful and I bless all that I see. Do not judge by appearances, but judge by right judgment—John 7:24.

Day Twenty-Four

Thank you nose. Thank you for smelling the flowers, the ocean, the rain soaked grass and dinner cooking. I am so grateful for you, nose. Thanks for helping me to breathe. You are a two-way street that exhales and inhales. You are so nice because you warm, moisten and filter the air that goes to my lungs. Your mucus catches dust, small particles and germs preventing them from getting to my lungs. I bless and thank my two nostrils, my hard palate, soft palate, my nasal cavity, the olfactory bulb, and my sinuses. I thank you nose because you help me to taste the foods that I eat. I appreciate you for all that you do. Love to you.

Affirmation: Today I am nosey. I keep my mind on my nose and show it love for all that it does for me. I have a healthy, beautiful good-smelling nose.

Day Twenty-Five

Bless mouth and my lips! Thank you lips for all the nerve endings that enable me to enjoy a kiss. Thanks for keeping food and water inside my mouth and for smiling. I love my lips. Thank you mouth for being big and wide open when I laugh.

Affirmation: Today I am kind to my lips. I decorate my lips with lipstick or chapstick or lip gloss. Today I kiss someone that I love. Today I use my lips to smile. Today I open my mouth and say whatever comes to mind.

.

❦

Day Twenty-Six

Thank you and bless you teeth and gums. Thank you for helping me bite into a crunchy apple. Thank you for helping me talk and sing. I love you crown, dentin, pulp, root, cementum, gum and jawbones. I love and bless you teeth: canines, molars, premolars, and incisors.

If you have dentures, thank the ancient Etruscans who in 700 BC invented false teeth.

Affirmation: I take care of my teeth and gums. I brush my teeth morning, noon and night, use dental floss, chew sugarless gum, and see a dentist for regular checkups.

Day Twenty-Seven

I thank and bless you tongue. I thank you for helping me chew, swallow, taste, talk and sing. I thank you for fighting germs and for working even when I am asleep. You push saliva down my throat. You are pink and pretty. I love you tongue.

Look in the mirror and stick out your tongue, wiggle it and your nose. This is good exercise for both.

Affirmation: My tongue is healthy and limber. It is perfect, whole and complete.

Day Twenty-Eight

I thank and bless you ears. Thanks for helping me keep my balance dear ears. Thanks for bringing in sound. I love and bless all parts of you, the auricle, eardrum, hammer, anvil, stirrup, and earlobe. Thank you ears for bringing me the sound of birds chirping or a baby crying or the wind blowing or someone saying I love you.

If you have a problem hearing, thank goodness for hearing aids.

Affirmation: Today I hear with my ears and with my heart.

❧

Day Twenty-Nine

Thank you and bless you hair. I love each and every strand, every hair follicle, and each sebaceous gland. Thanks hair for the job you do on my head, in my nose, on my body. Thanks eyelashes for protecting my eyes. Thanks for protecting my ears.
If you burn your hair or in any way harm your hair, ask for its forgiveness.

If your hair is long and lovely or short and cute, love it and tell it that it is loved and appreciated. If you have no hair, be thankful for wigs, hair transplants or be thankfully bald. Bald heads can be scintillatingly erotic. Give thanks for your hair even if the hair is no longer there.

Affirmation:
My hair is a wonder. It does a wonderful job and I love it.

Day Thirty

Thank you and bless you brain. You are my mainframe power station. I am thankful for waking up and being, as the old ones used to say, clothed in my right mind. My brain is not my mind, but without a functioning brain, I might not know the difference.

Exercise the muscle of your brain. Work a crossword puzzle, play scrabble, draw a picture or read a book or play a video game. Use your imagination to think the most wonderful, loving, and positive thoughts.

Affirmation: I change my thinking and change my life. Today I think like a winner. I replace negative thoughts with positive ones. I think thoughts of peace, joy, and love.

Just because the thirty days are complete, do not forget to be forever grateful and thankful for the body in which you live. Everything responds to love and your body will too. Gratitude is a wonderful elixir.

I am grateful to you for reading this book and I hope that you will pass it along to someone else who may be feeling out of sorts or not in touch with her or his body.

Namaste,
Nagueyalti Warren